Special occasions and celebrations may be the right time for chic lobster; then again, one doesn't need much of an excuse, a plentiful catch or a craving for rich flavor will do, to cook up delicious lobster dishes. Take your cue from these unique recipes and turn out a top crustacean...

now you're cookin'
LOBSTER

THIS BOOK JUST MAKES YOU WANNA COOK.

REBO
PUBLISHERS

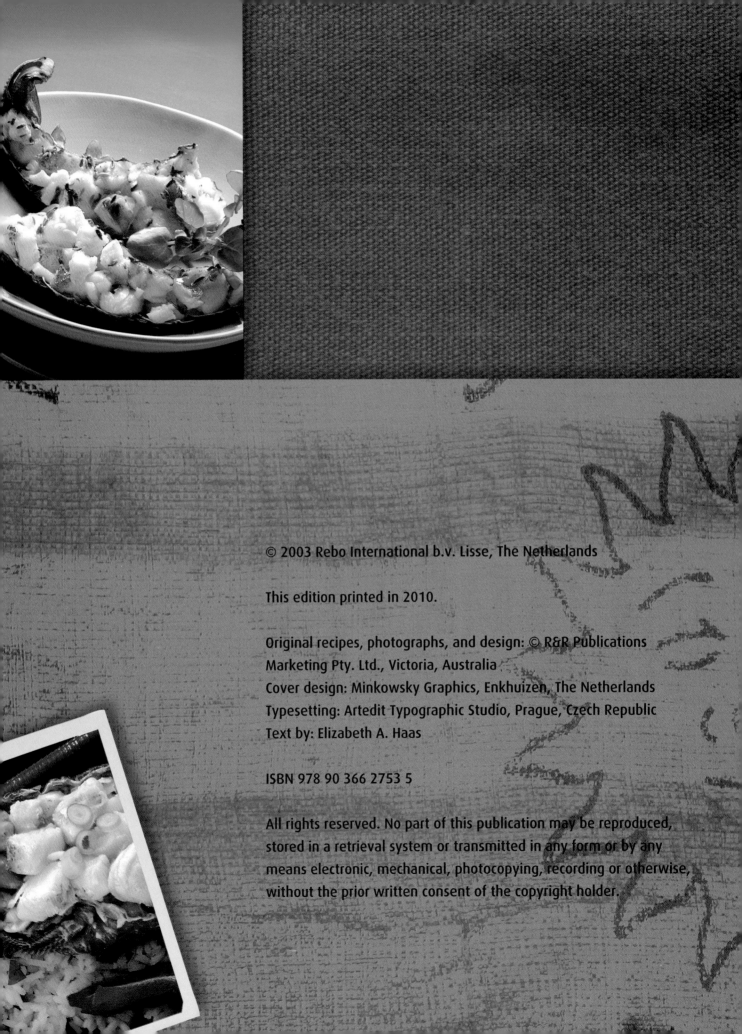

© 2003 Rebo International b.v. Lisse, The Netherlands

This edition printed in 2010.

Original recipes, photographs, and design: © R&R Publications
Marketing Pty. Ltd., Victoria, Australia
Cover design: Minkowsky Graphics, Enkhuizen, The Netherlands
Typesetting: Artedit Typographic Studio, Prague, Czech Republic
Text by: Elizabeth A. Haas

ISBN 978 90 366 2753 5

now you're cookin'
LOBSTER

Foreword

Lobster is chic. Very often it is the most expensive item on the menu when dining out. If you want to prepare something truly unique, and just a bit decadent, perhaps for a very special occasion, look no further than lobster. Your guests will applaud your kitchen skills as they savor this elegant delicacy.

You may need some courage as you prepare your lobster for the table; to transform a living lobster into a culinary wonder is not for the faint of heart. Boiled lobster may be the easiest for beginners who do not wish to cut up a live lobster with a knife. It has been said that you can "hypnotize" a lobster before boiling by rubbing the top of its abdomen or head.

This cookbook is devoted exclusively to lobster and offers countless variations for presenting the classic crustacean. From Lobster Flambé and Lobster Crepes to Creamy Lobster Bisque and Green Mango and Lobster Curry, the recipes here will bring a touch of sophistication and exquisite seafood flavor to your table.

U.S. KITCHEN CONVERSION
(LIQUID OR VOLUME, APPROXIMATE)

1 tsp. = 1/3 tbsp./5 ml
1 tbsp. = 1/2 fl. oz./15 ml
2 tbsp. = 1 fl. oz./30 ml
1/4 cup = 2 fl. oz./60 ml
1/3 cup = 2 2/3 fl. oz./80 ml
1/2 cup = 4 fl. oz./118 ml
2/3 cup = 5 1/3 fl. oz./158 ml
3/4 cup = 6 fl. oz./177 ml
7/8 cup = 7 fl. oz./207 ml
1 cup = 8 fl. oz./237 ml

Lobster Lemon and Dill Sauce

Serves 4

PREPARATION

Remove the lobster meat from the shell and cut into medallions
Melt the butter and saute garlic. Quickly add lobster and saute briskly.
Set aside and keep warm.

Now add sherry and dill to the pan and reduce liquid by half.
Add the fish stock, again reducing by half. Turn heat to medium
and add the cream, tomato paste, salt and pepper and simmer
for approximately 5 minutes.

Return lobster meat to the pan together with its juices
and add lemon juice to taste. Serve over hot pasta cooked
al dente and garnish with chopped dill.

INGREDIENTS

1 1/2 lb. (500 g) spaghetti, boiled and drained
4 green lobster tails
1/3 cup (85 g) butter
1 large clove garlic, crushed
1/2 cup (4 fl. oz/120 ml) sherry
2 tbsp. fresh dill, chopped
3/4 cup (6 fl. oz./150 ml) fish stock
1 2/3 cups (10 fl. oz./300 ml) cream
2 tbsp. tomato paste

salt to taste
freshly ground black pepper
juice of 1/2 lemon
extra fresh dill, chopped

Lobster Crepes

INGREDIENTS
FILLING

2 cups (290 g) lobster meat, fresh or frozen

1/4 cup (60 g) butter

2 tbsp. onion, chopped, 2 cups mushrooms, sliced

1/4 cup (30 g) flour

1/2 tbsp. salt

1/8 tsp. pepper

1 1/2 cup (12 fl. oz./357 ml) milk

1/4 cup (2 fl. oz/60 ml) butter, melted

1/4 cup (60 g) Swiss cheese, grated

CREPES

2 eggs, 3/4 cup (85 g) flour

1/2 tsp. salt

1 tsp. dried parsley

1 tsp. dried chives

1 cup (8 fl. oz./237 ml) milk

PREPARATION

If frozen, thaw and chop lobster into bite sized pieces. Melt butter and saute onions and mushrooms, 3–5 minutes. Stir in flour and seasonings; add milk and cook, stirring constantly until thickened. Add lobster.

Beat eggs, add flour and seasonings. Add milk and beat until smooth. Refrigerate 2 hours. For each crepe, pour 2–3 tablespoons of batter in a heated, oiled pan. Brown lightly on each side.

Spoon 3 tablespoons of filling into each crepe, roll up and arrange in a baking dish. Brush with half the melted butter and sprinkle with grated Swiss cheese. Bake at 425°F (220°C) for 5–8 minutes. Stir remaining melted butter into remaining filling and serve over crepes.

Green Mango and Lobster Curry

Serves 4

PREPARATION

Place coconut cream, curry paste, lemon grass, and lime leaves
in a saucepan and bring to the boil, reduce heat and simmer
for 5 minutes or until fragrant.

Add mango and simmer for 3 minutes. Add lobster, sugar, and fish sauce
and simmer for 7–8 minutes or until lobster is cooked.
Stir in vinegar and cilantro.

INGREDIENTS

1 1/2 cups (12 fl. oz/357 ml) coconut cream
1 tsp. Thai green curry paste
1 stalk fresh lemon grass, bruised or
1/2 tsp. dried lemon grass, soaked
 in hot water until soft
4 kaffir lime leaves, finely sliced
1 large green (unripe) mango,
 cut into 1/4-inch-thick (5 mm) slices
1 lb. (500 g) lobster meat,
 cut into 2-inch (5 cm) cubes

1 tbsp. palm or brown sugar
2 tbsp. Thai fish sauce (nam pla)
1 tbsp. coconut vinegar
2 oz. (60 g) fresh cilantro
leaves

Chinese Lobster Stir Fry

PREPARATION

If frozen, thaw and chop lobster into bite size pieces. In a skillet saute lobster and garlic in oil for 1 minute. Add broth and vegetables and simmer uncovered for 5 minutes. Season with salt and pepper.

INGREDIENTS

2 cups (290 g) lobster meat,
fresh or frozen
2 tbsp. oil
1 small clove garlic, minced
1/2 cup (4 fl. oz./120 ml) chicken broth
1 small red bell pepper, sliced
1 cup (33 g) bean sprouts
1 cup (124 g) water chestnuts
1 cup (70g) broccoli
1 1/2 cups (70 g) Chinese cabbage, shredded

1/2 tsp. salt
1/4 tsp. pepper
1 egg, beaten

Lobster Bisque

14

INGREDIENTS

1 small lobster, cooked
1 large carrot, peeled and diced
1 small onion, finely chopped
1/2 cup (120 g) butter
3/4 cup (6 fl. oz./177 ml) dry
white wine
bouquet garni
6 1/2 cups (3 1/4 pt./1 1/2 l) fish
or chicken stock
3/4 cup (145 g) rice

salt, pepper, and ground cayenne
1/2 cup (4 fl. oz./120 ml) cream
2 tbsp. brandy
chopped parsley

PREPARATION

Split the lobster in halves, lengthwise, and remove the flesh from the shell. Set aside. Wrap the shell in an old tea towel, crush with a hammer, and set aside. Saute the carrot and onion in half the butter until softened without coloring, about 5 minutes. Add the crushed shell, saute a further minute or so then add the wine. Boil hard until reduced by half. Add the bouquet garni, stock, and the rice.

After about 20 minutes, when the rice is tender, remove the large pieces of shell and bouquet garni. Puree in a food processor with the remainder of the batter, doing so in small batches. Pour through a strainer. Rinse out the food processor to remove every trace of shell and puree the strained liquid again, this time with the lobster flesh, saving a few pieces for the garnish. Reheat gently.

Add salt, pepper, and cayenne to taste then stir in the cream, brandy, and reserved lobster pieces cut into thin slices. Serve very hot garnished with parsley.

Lobster
Rice Salad

Serves 6

PREPARATION

Combine all ingredients. Place in a bowl or mold.

Chill for several hours. Turn out onto a bed of lettuce.

INGREDIENTS

3/4 cup (100 g) lobster meat, diced
2 cups (372 g) cooked rice
1 tbsp. lemon juice
1 cup (120 g) celery, finely diced
1/4 cup (37 g) green pepper, finely diced
1/2 cup (97 g) crushed pineapple, drained
1 tsp. salt
1/2 tsp. pepper
1/2 cup (4 fl. oz./120 ml) mayonnaise

Creamy Lobster Chowder

Serves 4–6

INGREDIENTS

1 1/2 cups (218 g) lobster meat, diced
1/4 cup (50 g) rice
1 tsp. salt
1/4 tsp. pepper
1/4 tsp. paprika
1 tbsp. onion, finely minced,
1 small red bell pepper, diced
2 stalks celery, chopped
2 cups (1 pt./473 ml) milk
2 cups (1 pt./473 ml) light cream

2 tbsp. butter
2 tbsp. chopped parsley

PREPARATION

Combine rice, salt, pepper, paprika, onion, capsicum, celery, milk, and cream in a saucepan. Cook over medium heat, stirring frequently, for 10–12 minutes, or until the rice softens.

Stir in the lobster, parsley, and butter. Remove from heat, cool, and store in the refrigerator. Just before serving, reheat the chowder over medium heat, stirring frequently.

King Island Lobster with Summer Herbs

PREPARATION

Immerse the lobster in boiling court bouillon for approximately 6 minutes. Drain and allow to cool, keeping lobster ¾ cooked. Remove meat from the shell keeping the tail intact; extract all the meat from the joints and legs. Slice lobster tail into medallions, season with salt and pepper and a little olive oil. Dice the meat from the legs along with the end pieces of the tail finely. Lightly grill the lobster medallions. Slice the cooked potatoes while still warm into small rounds. Pick the chervil and tarragon, chop the chives. Blanch, peel, and deseed tomatotes, reserve enough for two tomato rounds and dice the remaining along with the avocado, add this to the chopped chives and chopped lobster and season. Mound the mixture into the middle of the plate; garnish with strips of green mango, tomato, and cucumber. Top with the grilled lobster medallions and potatoes. Dress lettuce and place on top of the avocado mixture; sprinkle with chervil and tarragon. Drizzle the lobster slices with crustacean oil, garnish with lobster tuilles and serve.

LOBSTER TUILLE

Reduce the lobster stock to a syrupy consistency–approximately cup (3 fl. oz/90 ml). Combine the flour and butter to form a paste. Mix in the reduction, salt, pepper, and the egg white a little at a time. Spread onto a greased tray as a sheet or through a stencil, sprinkle with sesame seeds, and bake at 350°F (180°C) until golden brown, approx 10 minutes.

INGREDIENTS

1 x 1 lb. (400 g) lobster
6 x lobster tuilles
1/2 piece green mango
2 tomatoes, 1/4 avocado
pinch chervil, chives, and tarragon
2 small potatoes, cooked and peeled
4 tbsp. crustacean oil
salt and pepper
2 tbsp. olive oil
1/2 cup (30 g) mixed seasonal lettuce
6 slices cucumber, skin removed

LOBSTER TUILLE

1 cup (8 fl. oz/237 ml) lobster stock
4 1/2 tbsp. flour
2 tbsp. butter
1 egg white
dash lemon juice
sesame seeds

Lobster Cheese Rolls

Serves 6

PREPARATION

Combine first 9 ingredients and toss lightly.
Top one half of each roll with the lobster mixture
and cover with the other roll half.

Wrap in aluminum foil and place in a 350°F (220°C)
oven for 8–10 minutes.

INGREDIENTS

1/2 cup (60 g) celery, chopped
2 tbsp. onion, minced
1/2 cup (4 fl. oz./120 ml) mayonnaise
1 tbsp. French dressing
1/2 cup (60 g) Cheddar cheese,
grated, 1/3 cup (40 g) slivered
almonds, toasted
2 tsp. lemon juice
1/2 tsp. salt
2 cups (290 g) sliced, cooked lobster
meat, 6 buttered rolls

Lobster Toasts

PREPARATION

Combine all ingredients (except toast) in a food processor and blend until creamy.

Spread on toast and heat through under preheated hot grill before serving.

Sprinkle with chopped parsley and ground pepper, drizzle with some olive oil and serve.

INGREDIENTS

12 slices of baguette, or Turkish bread, toasted

1 cup (8 fl. oz./237 ml) cream cheese

1/4 cup (60 g) cooked lobster meat

1 tbsp. olive oil

juice of 1/2 lemon

salt and pepper, to taste

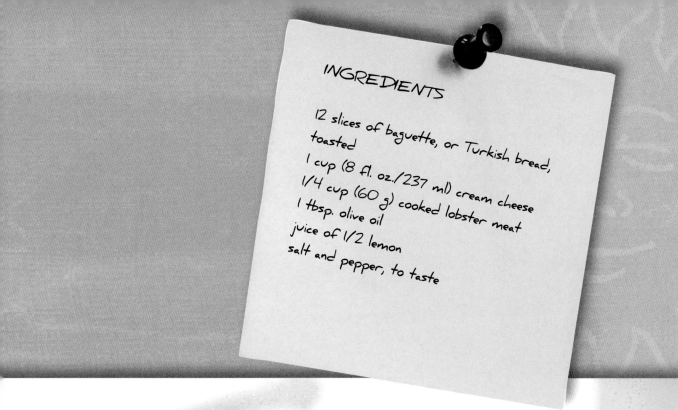

Lobster Pineapple Salad

Serves 6-8

PREPARATION

Dice lobster, reserving the juice. Break the fish filets into chunks. Combine lobster, juice, and fish filets, cover, and refrigerate for 10–12 hours.

Drain seafood well and add remaining ingredients. Toss lighty and serve on a bed of lettuce or hollowed out pineapple halves.

INGREDIENTS

2 cups (290 g) cooked lobster meat
2 fish filets (about 180 g each), cooked
1 cup (120 g) celery, chopped
1/2 cup (70 g) almonds, chopped
1 1/2 cups (271 g) pineapple chunks
3/4 cup (6 fl. oz/177 ml) mayonnaise
1 tsp. curry powder
1/2 tsp. salt

Sea Captain's Dip

Makes 2 cups

PREPARATION

Cream the cream cheese and lemon juice.
Add mayonnaise, garlic salt, onion,
chives and lobster. Mix well.

Chill at least 6 hours, then serve with crackers
or fresh vegetables.

INGREDIENTS

3/4 cup (109 g) lobster meat, finely diced

1 x 4 oz. (125 g) package cream cheese

2 tbsp. lemon juice

1/4 cup (2 fl. oz./60 ml) mayonnaise

1/4 tsp. garlic salt

2 tbsp. onion, diced

1 tsp. dried chives

Lobster Filo Triangles

Makes 24

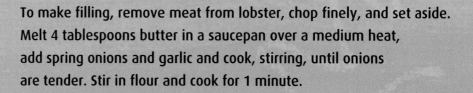

PREPARATION

To make filling, remove meat from lobster, chop finely, and set aside.
Melt 4 tablespoons butter in a saucepan over a medium heat,
add spring onions and garlic and cook, stirring, until onions
are tender. Stir in flour and cook for 1 minute.

Remove pan from heat and whisk in wine and cream, a little at a time,
until well blended. Season to taste with cayenne and black pepper,
return to heat and cook, stirring constantly, until sauce boils
and thickens. Reduce heat to low and simmer for 3 minutes.
Remove from heat, stir in lobster meat and cool completely.

Cut pastry sheets lengthwise into 2–inch–wide (5 cm) strips.
Working with one strip of pastry at a time, brush pastry
with melted butter. Place a teaspoonful of the filling on one end
of strip, fold corner of pastry diagonally over filling,
then continue folding up the strip to make a neat triangle.

Place triangles on a baking tray, brush with butter
and bake for 10–15 minutes or until golden.

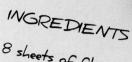

INGREDIENTS

8 sheets of filo pastry
1/2 cup (4 fl. oz./120 ml) butter,
melted and cooled

LOBSTER CREAM FILLING

1 cooked lobster
4 tbsp. butter
6 spring onions, chopped
2 cloves garlic, crushed
1 1/2 tbsp. flour

1/4 cup (2 fl. oz./60 ml) white
wine
1/4 cup (2 fl. oz./60 ml) double
cream
pinch cayenne pepper
freshly ground black pepper

31

Stuffed Spiny Lobster

Serves 4

PREPARATION

Soak the cloud ear for 1 hour. Cut the lobster in half lengthwise and remove the meat, reserving the shells. Cut the meat into 8 equal portions and drop in boiling water. When the surface of the meat whitens, immediately drain and plunge into ice water. Drain again and wipe dry.

Wash the shells thoroughly and boil in lightly salted water until they turn red. Cut the shiitake (or brown) mushrooms into thin strips. Cut the cloud ear, carrot, and asparagus into 1 ½–inch–long (4 cm) slivers. Preheat the oven to 440°F (200°C).

Combine the bonito stock and all the vegetables in a soup pot and bring to a boil over high heat. Season with soy sauce and mirin and boil for about 3 minutes until the vegetables are just tender. Pour in the beaten egg in a circular motion to cover, and stir gently. Cover with a plate which fits down inside the pan and sits directly onto the food and turn off the heat (this ensures even heat and flavor distribution by forcing the rising heat down). Let stand for 2–3 minutes and then drain.

Return the lobster to the shells. Top with the egg mixture and place in the preheated oven. When the surface of the egg mixture is lightly browned, remove the lobster from oven, transfer to plates, and serve.

INGREDIENTS

1 dried cloud ear mushroom
2 live (1 lb./450 g) spiny lobsters
4 fresh shiitake mushrooms, washed
and stems removed, or 4 fresh brown
mushrooms, washed and trimmed
1/4 medium carrot
2 stalks green asparagus, trimmed
7 tbsp. bonito stock (dashi)
1 tbsp. light soy sauce
1 tbsp. mirin
3 eggs, lightly beaten

Lobster
in Mint Pesto

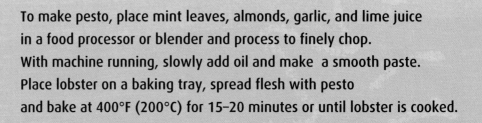

PREPARATION

To make pesto, place mint leaves, almonds, garlic, and lime juice
in a food processor or blender and process to finely chop.
With machine running, slowly add oil and make a smooth paste.
Place lobster on a baking tray, spread flesh with pesto
and bake at 400°F (200°C) for 15–20 minutes or until lobster is cooked.

SERVING SUGGESTION

This dish is perfect for a special occasion meal. Start with an antipasto
platter–purchase the ingredients from the delicatessen section
of your supermarket. Accompany lobster with boiled new potatoes
tossed with olive oil and black pepper and a salad of assorted lettuces
and chopped fresh herbs. Finish the meal with a good quality purchased
ice cream topped with a tablespoon of your favorite liqueur.

INGREDIENTS

2 uncooked lobster tails,
halved lengthwise

MINT PESTO

1 bunch fresh mint
4 tbsp. almonds, toasted
1 clove garlic, crushed
1/4 cup (2 fl. oz./60 ml) lime juice
1/4 cup (2 fl. oz./60 ml) olive oil

35

Garlic Lobster Tails with Exotic Salad

Serves 4–6

INGREDIENTS

6 green (raw) lobster tails
1/3 cup (80 g) butter, softened
2 tsp. crushed garlic
2 tsp. Honey and Lemon Marinade
(below)

EXOTIC SALAD

1 avocado, cut into 1/4-inch (1/2 cm) dice
2 Lebanese cucumbers, diced
1/2 small rock melon, peeled and diced
1/3 cup (3 fl. oz./80 ml) Honey and
Lemon Marinade

HONEY & LEMON MARINADE

1/2 cup (4 fl. oz./120 ml) olive oil
2 tbsp. lemon juice, 1 tbsp. honey,
1 tbsp. freshly crushed garlic,
2 bay leaves, crushed

PREPARATION

With kitchen scissors, cut each side of the soft shell on the underside of the lobster tails, and remove. Run a metal skewer through the length of each tail to keep them flat while cooking. Soften the butter and mix in the garlic and marinade. Spread a coating on the lobster meat.

Prepare salad before commencing to cook lobster tails. Mix the diced avocado, cucumber, and rock melon together. Pour the marinade over the salad. Refrigerate until needed.

Heat the barbecue to medium-high and oil the grill bars. Place lobster tails shell-side down and cook until shell turns red. Spread with more butter and turn meat-side down and cook for 5–8 minutes or meat turns white. Turn again and cook 2 minutes more shell-side down. Remove skewers and place on warm plates. Dot with any remaining butter mixture and serve immediately with exotic salad.

Grilled Creamy
Lobster

Serves 6

PREPARATION

Halve the lobsters lengthwise and remove meat; cut into chunks.
Melt the butter and saute the onions until tender. Add the flour
and stir over a low heat for 2 minutes. Gradually add the milk
and allow the sauce to thicken. Add the liqueur and simmer
for 2 minutes then stir in the cheese and mustards.

Spoon a little of the sauce into the lobster shells, add the lobster
and coat with the remaining sauce. Sprinkle with breadcrumbs
and dot with butter. Grill until brown and bubbling. Serve immediately.

INGREDIENTS

3 medium, cooked lobsters
3 tbsp. butter or margarine
1 small onion, chopped
3 tbsp. flour
1 1/2 cups (12 fl. oz./355 ml) milk
3 tbsp. cherry liqueur
2 tbsp. grated mild Cheddar cheese
2 tsp. French mustard
1/2 tsp. English mustard
breadcrumbs
butter

Grilled Lobster with Chili Salsa

Serves 2

INGREDIENTS

2 lobsters (about 12 oz./35 g each),
cooked
4 tsp. olive oil
cayenne pepper

FOR THE SALSA

2 tbsp. olive oil
1 red bell pepper, deseeded
and diced

1 small onion, chopped
1 large red chili, deseeded
and finely chopped
1 tbsp. sun-dried tomato puree
salt and black pepper

PREPARATION

To make the salsa, heat the oil in a saucepan and fry the red pepper, onion and, chili for 5 minutes or until tender. Stir in the tomato puree and season to taste. Transfer to a bowl.

To cut the lobsters in half lengthways, turn one on its back. Cut through the head end first, using a large, sharp knife, then turn the lobster around and cut through the tail end. Discard the small greyish "sac" in the head: everything else in the shell is edible. Crack the large claws with a small hammer or wooden rolling pin. Repeat with the second lobster. Drizzle the cut side of the lobsters with the oil and sprinkle with the cayenne pepper.

Heat a large non-stick frying pan or ridged cast iron grill pan until very hot, then add the lobster halves, cut-side down, and cook for 2–3 minutes, until lightly golden. Serve with the salsa.

Lobster Topping

42

Serves 6–8

PREPARATION

Beat together cream cheese, mayonnaise, and sour cream.
Add lobster juice, lemon juice, garlic, and chives.

Beat well. Stir in lobster.
Serve over hot baked potatoes.

INGREDIENTS

1 cup (145 g) lobster meat, diced
1 x 4 oz. (125 g) package cream cheese
1/2 cup (4 fl. oz/120 ml) mayonnaise
1/4 cup (2 fl. oz./60 ml) sour cream
2 tbsp. lobster juice
2 tsp. lemon juice
1/2 clove garlic, crushed
1 tsp. dried chives

43

Lobster and Scallop Supreme

Serves 4

PREPARATION

Cook rice in boiling salted water for 12–15 minutes. Drain and keep warm. Halve the lobster lengthwise and remove the digestive tract. Chop flesh into bite size pieces. Melt 1 tablespoon of the butter in a frying pan with the lemon juice and saute scallops and shallots until just tender.

Add the lobster and allow to heat through. Toss parsley and remaining butter through rice and spoon onto a heated serving plate. Spoon the seafood mixture into the shells and serve with the rice.

INGREDIENTS

2 cups rice
2 lb. (1 kg) lobster
3 tbsp. butter or margarine
2 tbsp. lemon juice
1 1/2 lb. (75 g) scallops
6 shallots, chopped
1 tbsp. chopped parsley

Lobster Cheese Casserole

Serves 4-6

PREPARATION

Place lobster in a greased 1 quart (1 liter) casserole.
Over low heat, melt butter, blend in flour,
and slowly add milk and cream.

Cook, stirring constantly until mixture is thick
and smooth. Add the ½ cup (57 g) cheese,
salt and gren pepper. Stir until cheese melts.
Pour over lobster.

Sprinkle ¼ cup (30 g) cheese over top
and garnish with paprika.
Bake at 350°F (180°C) for 15 minutes.
Broil for 2 minutes to brown the top.

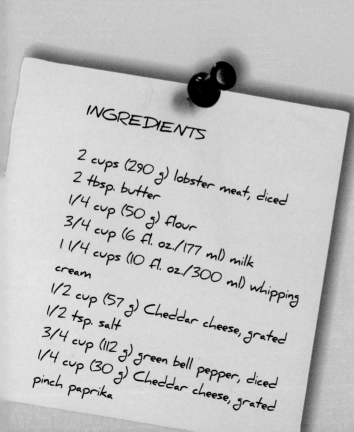

INGREDIENTS

2 cups (290 g) lobster meat, diced
2 tbsp. butter
1/4 cup (50 g) flour
3/4 cup (6 fl. oz./177 ml) milk
1 1/4 cups (10 fl. oz./300 ml) whipping cream
1/2 cup (57 g) Cheddar cheese, grated
1/2 tsp. salt
3/4 cup (112 g) green bell pepper, diced
1/4 cup (30 g) Cheddar cheese, grated
pinch paprika

Liz's Lobster

Serves 2

PREPARATION

Simmer lobster tails in white wine until tender. Remove lobster from wine and set aside. Reduce wine down to a cup.

Melt butter in a saucepan, add flour, and cook for 1 minute. Gradually add wine and stir until sauce thickens. Add all remaining ingredients and stir until sauce is simmering. Remove from heat.

Place lobster tails on top of a bed of rice and top with sauce. Garnish with fresh asparagus.

INGREDIENTS

2 medium lobster tails
2 cups (1 pt./473 ml) dry white wine
3 tbsp. flour
3 tbsp. butter
1/2 cup (4 fl. oz./120 ml) cream
1 tsp. lemon juice
1/2 tsp. Dijon mustard
1 tbsp. capers

Grilled Lobster and Lemon-Anisette Butter

Serves 6

PREPARATION

Melt the butter in a saucepan and add the lemon juice, Pernod, and dill. Stir well over medium heat and set to one side. Cut the lobster tails in half removing, the meat and cut ting into chunks, then return to the shell.

Place the tails on a grilling rack, brush liberally with the butter, and place under the grill. Grill, brushing regularly with the butter until cooked. Serve with a tossed mixed lettuce and watercress salad.

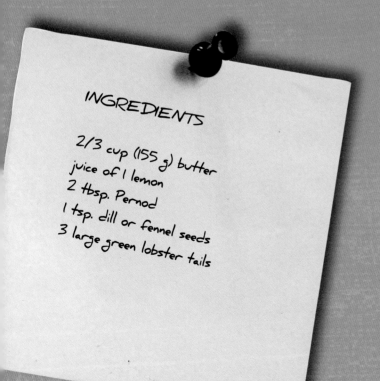

INGREDIENTS

2/3 cup (155 g) butter
juice of 1 lemon
2 tbsp. Pernod
1 tsp. dill or fennel seeds
3 large green lobster tails

Lobster
à L'Americane

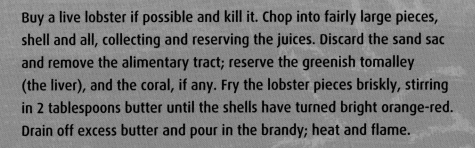

PREPARATION

Buy a live lobster if possible and kill it. Chop into fairly large pieces, shell and all, collecting and reserving the juices. Discard the sand sac and remove the alimentary tract; reserve the greenish tomalley (the liver), and the coral, if any. Fry the lobster pieces briskly, stirring in 2 tablespoons butter until the shells have turned bright orange-red. Drain off excess butter and pour in the brandy; heat and flame.

Peel and finely chop the shallots, sweat in 3 tablespoons butter in a wide, fairly deep pan; add the white wine and continue cooking until this has evaporated. Add the lobster pieces, their reserved juice and the hot fish stock. Add the blanched, peeled, seeded, and chopped tomatoes and the sprig of tarragon. Simmer for 15 minutes. Work the coral into 3 ½ tablespoons butter softened at room temperature. Remove the lobster pieces with a slotted spoon or ladle and place in a heated serving dish. Discard the tarragon. Add the coral butter to the sauce in the pan, stir gently as the butter melts, and add the chopped parsley. Season to taste with salt and freshly ground pepper.
Pour over the lobster and serve at once.

INGREDIENTS

1 lobster (about 2 1/2 lb./1 kg)
2 tbsp. olive oil
1/2 cup (4 fl. oz./120 g) butter
brandy
6 shallots
7/8 cup (7 fl. oz./207 ml) dry white wine
7/8 cup (7 fl. oz./207 ml) fish stock (fumet)
4 fresh or tinned tomatoes
1 sprig tarragon
1 tbsp. finely chopped parsley
salt and pepper

Lobster and Sprout Salad

Serves 4–6

PREPARATION

Combine the Pernod, mayonnaise, sorrel, celery, and chili sauce.

Chop the lobster into bite size pieces and arrange over the pea sprouts. Spoon over the sauce. Serve with thin slices of buttered wholemeal bread.

INGREDIENTS

1/4 cup (2 fl. oz./60 ml) Pernod

1 1/2 cup (12 fl. oz./357 ml) mayonnaise

4 large sorrel leaves, finely shredded

1/4 cup (30 g) celery, finely chopped

1/4 tsp. chili sauce

1 lb. (500 g) cooked lobster

snowpea sprouts

Lobster-Stuffed Potatoes

Serves 6

PREPARATION

Preheat oven to 375°F (190°C).
Cut baked potatoes in half lengthwise and carefully scoop
out insides, reserving the skins.

In a bowl, mash the potato, then add butter, sour cream, onion,
and pepper. Beat until smooth. Fold in lobster meat and mushrooms,
and place mixture back in the 12 potato skin halves.
Sprinkle with grated cheese and place on a baking sheet.
Bake 15–20 minutes, or until potatoes are heated through.

INGREDIENTS

1/2 cup (73 g) lobster meat, diced
6 potatoes, baked
1 tbsp. butter
1/2 cup (4 fl. oz./120 ml) sour cream
1/4 cup (40 g) onion, grated
1/4 tsp. pepper
1/4 cup (18 g) mushrooms, diced
1/2 cup (30 g) Cheddar cheese, grated

Lobster with Apples and Calvados

Makes 2 generous portions

PREPARATION

Use a firm variety of apple that will not disintegrate when cooked. Cut the carrot into small pieces, the leek into rings, and chop the onion coarsely; place in a deep, non-metallic saucepan. Remove the core from 1 apple but do not peel; cut into small pieces and add to the saucepan. Add all but 3 ½ fl. oz. (100 ml) of the cider and season with salt and a little freshly ground white or black pepper. Bring to the boil and boil for 2 minutes. If you are using a live lobster, add it to the fast boiling liquid now; cover and cook for 10 minutes. Peel, core, and thinly slice the remaining apples and use to cover the bottom of a wide, shallow ovenproof dish. Sprinkle with the well drained sultanas. Spoon half the cream and the remaining cider over the apples. Place in the oven, preheated to 400°F (200°C) uncovered, for 10 minutes.

Drain the lobster. Boil the cider stock fast until reduced to about 1 pint (600 ml); draw aside from the heat and when it has cooled a little, liquify until smooth. Return to the saucepan with the rest of the cream and the Calvados and boil over a moderate heat until it has reduced further and thickened slightly. Remove from heat; beat in the butter a small piece at a time. Add salt and freshly ground pepper to taste. If you have cooked the lobster in the cider, cut lengthwise in half at this point. If you have bought your lobster ready cooked, place cut sides down on top of the apple slices for their last 5 minutes' baking in the oven to warm through and take up a little of the apple and cider flavor. Remove and discard the small legs and antennae, the stomach sac, spongy gills, and intestinal tract. Place each half on a heated plate; arrange the baked apple slices and sultanas on top, and coat with the sauce.

INGREDIENTS

1 lobster (about 2 1/2 lb./1 kg)
1 small carrot
1 leek, 1 small onion
3 apples
2 1/2 pt. (1 1/2 l) dry cider
2 tbsp. sultanas, soaked in water
3 tbsp. double cream
1 1/2 tbsp. Calvados or applejack
3 1/2 tbsp. unsalted butter
salt and pepper

Lobster Bordelaise

PREPARATION

A live crawfish or lobster is traditional for this dish. Use a cleaver or sharp, heavy kitchen knife to cut off the head and slice the body into "steaks", cutting through the shell where the rings are jointed together. Remove and discard the black intestinal tract and the sand sac or stomach (found in the head). Crush the thin legs, collecting the juice which runs out and place in a bowl, together with the liver; reserve the coral if you have a hen (female) lobster.

Heat 2 tablespoons oil in a large, deep pan with 2 tablespoons butter; add the slices of lobster (still in the shell) and fry briskly until the shell is red. Transfer to a very hot flameproof dish, pour the heated brandy over them, and flame. Add the cleaned, prepared, and finely chopped vegetables to the oil, butter, and juices left in the pan and fry gently until tender, then pour in the wine, the juice from the lobster, tomato puree, bouquet garni, salt and freshly ground pepper. Simmer for 15 minutes, discard the bouquet garni, and liquify the sauce. Return to the pan and add the lobster pieces; cook gently for 10 minutes. Weight the coral if present, then weigh out an equal amount of butter softened at room temperature and work the coral into it; add 2 tablespoons of the sauce from the pan and mix well, then stir into the saucepan. Cook over the lowest possible heat for 10 minutes more. Serve the lobster pieces coated with sauce and surrounded by small triangles or shapes of bread, toasted or lightly fried in butter.

INGREDIENTS

1 crawfish or lobster (about 2 1/2 lb./1 kg)
2 tbsp. olive oil, 3 1/2 tbsp. butter
3 tbsp. good brandy
1 onion, 1 carrot
1 small, white celery heart
2 cloves garlic, 2 shallots
1 1/4 cup (10 fl. oz./300 ml) red Bordeaux wine
2 tbsp. tomato puree
1 bouquet garni, few sprigs parsley
8 triangles white bread
salt and pepper

Lobster with Dill

PREPARATION

Prepare the lobsters for cooking and add to a very large pan of boiling, slightly salted water; cook for 15–20 minutes. Drain, take all the meat out of the shells and claws and dice.

Wash and dry the dill weed, snip off the small feathery leaves, reserving a sprig or two for decoration. Wash and dry the lettuce.
Drain the pineapple well and cut into small pieces.
Slice the mushrooms wafer thin.

Place all the ingredients except the lettuce and dill in a bowl and mix with the mayonnaise, then fold in the lightly beaten cream, flavored with a pinch of sugar, salt and freshly ground white pepper.

Line a large salad bowl with the lettuce leaves; spoon in the lobster mixture and decorate with the reserved dill sprigs.

INGREDIENTS

2 lobsters (about 1 1/2 lb./770 g each)
3 sprigs dill
1 lettuce
2 slices fresh or unsweetened canned pineapple
3 1/2 oz. (100 g) button mushrooms
1 tbsp. mayonnaise
7/8 cup (7 fl. oz./200ml) whipping cream
pinch sugar
salt and pepper

Lobster Abegweit

Serves 6

PREPARATION

Melt butter, add lobster meat and saute for 5 minutes.

Add mushrooms and onion, and saute an additional 5 minutes.
Stir in flour, salt, evaporated milk, and whole milk. Cook, stirring
constantly until thick and smooth. Stir in cheese spread and parsley.

Serve over patty shells. Toss through hot cooked pasta and serve.

INGREDIENTS

2 cups (290 g) lobster meat, diced
3 tbsp. butter
1 cup (70 g) mushrooms, sliced
1 tbsp. onion, diced
3 tbsp. flour
1 tsp. salt
1 1/2 cups (12 fl. oz./316 ml) evaporated milk
1/2 cup (4 fl. oz./120 ml) whole milk
1/4 cup (2 fl. oz./60 ml) processed cheese spread
2 tbsp. parsely, chooped

65

Lobster Crowns

PREPARATION

Remove stems from mushrooms. Sprinkle caps with salt and pepper and fry for 5 minutes in butter over medium heat. Combine onion, mushroom stems, butter, and lobster. Stuff caps with the mixture, and sprinkle with grated cheese.
Broil for 4–5 minutes.

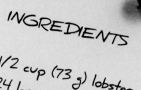

INGREDIENTS

1/2 cup (73 g) lobster, diced
24 large mushrooms
1/4 tsp. salt
dash pepper
2 tbsp. butter
1 tbsp. onion, finely diced
2 tbsp. mushroom stems, finely diced
1 tsp. butter
1/2 cup (57 g) Cheddar cheese, grated

Lobster
Croquettes

PREPARATION

Chop the meat of one large or two small lobsters,
add pepper, salt, and a little mace.

Mix with this about a quarter as much breadcrumbs as you have meat;
add enough melted butter to shape them into pointed balls.

Roll in beaten egg, then pulverized crackers, and fry in boiling lard.
Serve very hot garnished with the lobsters and parsley.
This is a delicious dish for luncheon or entree at dinner.

INGREDIENTS

1 big or two small lobsters
breadcrumbs
1 egg, beaten
butter, melted
salt, pepper, mace
pulverized crackers
1 tbsp. of finely chopped parsley

Creamy Lobster with Asparagus

Serves 6

INGREDIENTS

3 medium lobsters, cooked
3 tbsp. butter or margarine
1 small onion, chopped
3 tbsp. flour
1/2 cup (4 fl. oz./120 ml) milk
3 tbsp. cherry liqueur
2 tbsp. grated mild Cheddar
2 tsp. French mustard
breadcrumbs
butter

1 large bunch of asparagus

PREPARATION

Cut the lobsters in half lengthwise and remove the meat and cut into pieces. Melt the butter and saute the onion until translucent. Add the flour and stir over low heat for 2 minutes. Pour the milk in gradually and let the sauce thicken. Add the liqueur and let it simmer, 2 minutes, then add the cheese and mustard.

Spoon a little sauce into the lobster shells, stuff the meat back into the shells and spread over remaining sauce. Sprinkle lobster meat with breadcrumbs and dot with butter. Set aside.

In the meantime, wash the asparagus spears and trim about 1 inch (2 1/2 cm) from the bottom of each spear. Tie the entire bunch with kitchen string and arrange upright in a tall, lidded pot. Pour in 2 inches (5 cm) of water. Bring to a boil then cover, cooking 2–8 minutes or until spears have turned bright green.

Grill the lobsters until they are brown and the meat is cooked through. Serve immediately with a side of steamed asparagus, drizzled with a little melted butter if you wish.

Lobster Lasagne

Serves 10–12

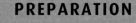

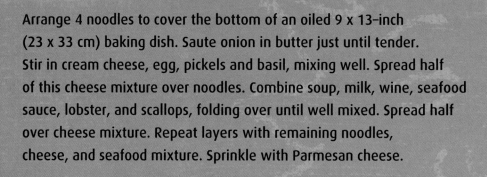

PREPARATION

Arrange 4 noodles to cover the bottom of an oiled 9 x 13-inch
(23 x 33 cm) baking dish. Saute onion in butter just until tender.
Stir in cream cheese, egg, pickels and basil, mixing well. Spread half
of this cheese mixture over noodles. Combine soup, milk, wine, seafood
sauce, lobster, and scallops, folding over until well mixed. Spread half
over cheese mixture. Repeat layers with remaining noodles,
cheese, and seafood mixture. Sprinkle with Parmesan cheese.

Bake, uncovered at 350°F (180°C) for 40 minutes or until
heated through. Sprinkle with mozzarella cheese
and bake 2–3 minutes longer or until cheese melts.
Remove from oven and let stand 15 minutes before serving.

INGREDIENTS

8 lasagne noodles, cooked and drained
1 cup (160 g) chopped onion
1 tbsp. butter
1 x 8 oz. (250 g) package cream cheese, softened
1 egg, beaten
1 1/4 cups (300 g) chopped dill pickles
2 tbsp. chopped basil
2 x 10 oz. (284 ml) cans cream of mushroom soup
1/2 cup (4 fl. oz./120 ml) milk
1/3 cup (3 fl. oz./80 ml) white wine or chicken broth
1/3 cup (3 fl. oz./80 ml) seafood sauce

1 x 11 oz. (320 g) can lobster meat, thawed and drained (several pieces of lobster meat can be set aside for a garnish, if desired)
1/2–3/4 lb. (250–275g) scallops, thaw if frozen and cut in half
1/3 cup (24 g) Parmesan cheese, grated
1 cup (112 g) mozzarella cheese, shredded

Lobster Flambé

PREPARATION

Rinse the lobsters under running cold water; dry with kitchen paper and cut lengthwise in half, using a strong, heavy kitchen knife.

Remove the sand sac in the head and the black thread running down the back (the intestinal tract). Season with salt and freshly ground pepper and generously brush all over the cut surface with melted butter.

Place on a very hot serving plate, heat 3 tablespoons brandy, pour over the lobsters and set alight.
Place on the table while still flaming.

INGREDIENTS

2 lobsters (about 1 1/4 lb./600 g each)
1/4 cup (57 g) butter
3 tbsp. brandy
salt and pepper

Sake-Simmered Lobster

Serves 4

PREPARATION

Cut the live lobsters in half lengthwise and then cut each half into 2–3 pieces. Cut the leeks into ½–inch (1 ½ cm) rounds, boil in salted water until just tender, and drain. Blanch the watercress in lightly salted boiling water, drain, and refresh in cold water. Drain again and cut into 1 ½–inch (4 cm) lengths. Slice the ginger with the grain into very fine slivers and soak in cold water for 2–3 minutes. Place the sake and water in a pan and bring to a boil over high heat, then add all the remaining simmering ingredients. Add the lobster and cover with a plate which fits down inside the pan and sits directly onto the food (this ensures even he at and flavor distribution by forcing the rising heat down). Boil for 5–6 minutes over high heat until the meat can be easily removed from the shell. Ladle simmering liquid over lobster several times. Add the leek and watercress. Heat through, add the ginger juice, and immediately remove from heat. Divide the lobster and vegetables among 4 bowls. Pour in an ample amount of sauce. Top with well drained ginger, garnish with chervil, and serve.

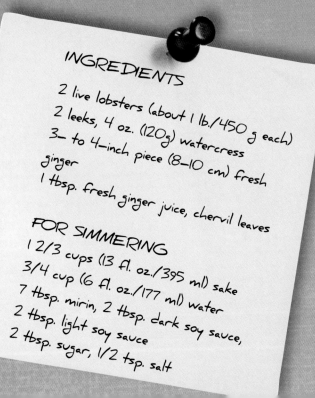

INGREDIENTS

2 live lobsters (about 1 lb./450 g each)
2 leeks, 4 oz. (120g) watercress
3– to 4–inch piece (8–10 cm) fresh ginger
1 tbsp. fresh ginger juice, chervil leaves

FOR SIMMERING

1 2/3 cups (13 fl. oz./395 ml) sake
3/4 cup (6 fl. oz./177 ml) water
7 tbsp. mirin, 2 tbsp. dark soy sauce,
2 tbsp. light soy sauce
2 tbsp. sugar, 1/2 tsp. salt

Lobster Mornay

PREPARATION

Remove lobster meat from shells and cut into bite-sized pieces. Reserve shells.

In a saucepan, place milk, bay leaf, onion, and peppercorns. Heat slowly to boiling point. Remove from heat, cover, and stand for 10 minutes. Strain.

In a pan: heat butter, and remove from heat. Stir in flour and blend, gradually adding strained milk. Return pan to heat, and stir constantly (until sauce boils and thickens). Simmer sauce for 1 minute. Remove from heat, add cream, cheese, salt and pepper. Stir sauce (until cheese melts), and add lobster.

Divide mixture between shells. Melt extra butter in a small pan, add breadcrumbs, and stir to combine.

Scatter crumbs over lobster and brown under a hot grill.

INGREDIENTS

1 medium lobster (cooked; halved)

MORNAY SAUCE

1 1/3 cup (11 fl. oz./310 ml) milk
1 bay leaf
1 small onion (chopped)
5 black peppercorns
2 tbsp. butter
2 tbsp. plain flour
2/3 cup cream to 1/4 cup (2 fl. oz./60ml)
cream

1/2 cup (60 g) cheese, grated
salt and pepper
3 tsp. butter (extra; melted)
2/3 cup (65 g) breadcrumbs
(fresh)

Surf and Turf Risotto

PREPARATION

Heat the olive oil and gently fry the garlic for a moment or two. Add the beef and saute until seared and crisp on both sides. Remove from the pan and keep warm wrapped in foil (for medium or well-done beef, bake at 392°F/200°C for 5 minutes or 10 minutes respectively, then keep warm wrapped in foil).

To the oil/garlic mixture, add the spring onions and bell pepper strips and saute until softened. Add the rice and stir to coat, then add the wine and simmer to evaporate the alcohol while the liquid is absorbed. When the rice mixture is firm, add the stock, half a cup at a time, stirring well after each addition and allowing each quantity of stock to be absorbed before the next addition. Continue in this fashion until the stock has all been incorporated. With the last addition of stock, add the lobster meat, cut into attractive, manageable pieces, and stir to distribute.

Peel and slice the onions. Either deep fry at 350°F (180°C) until crisp and golden, or alternatively, toss with 2 tablespoons olive oil and bake at 425°F (220°C) for 30–40 minutes, tossing frequently, until golden. Set aside until the risotto is finished and ready to serve. When almost all of the liquid has been absorbed and the rice is "al dente", stir through the Parmesan cheese, parsley, and sour cream. Meanwhile, remove the warm meat from the foil and thinly slice. Serve the risotto in individual bowls, fan out the meat and place on top of the risotto. Garnish with the crispy fried (or baked) onions and serve immediately.

INGREDIENTS

2 tbsp. olive oil

2 x 7 oz. (200 g) pieces of eye filet

4 cloves garlic

10 spring onions, chopped

1 red bell pepper, sliced into strips

2 cups (400 g) arborio rice

2/3 cup (5 fl. oz./150 ml) dry white wine

1 1/2 pt. (900 ml) rich vegetable or chicken stock, simmering

2 lobster tails, cooked

1 tbsp. Parmesan cheese, grated

1 tbsp. sour cream

lots of fresh parsley, chopped

2 onions, peeled and sliced

oil for frying

Lobster Provençale

Serves 4

PREPARATION

In a shallow frypan, melt butter over a moderate heat.
Add garlic, spring onions, tomatoes, salt and pepper, and saffron.
Cook until onions are translucent, about 2 minutes.

Remove meat from lobster, and cut into large pieces.
Add lobster to frypan, and flame with the brandy.
Cook gently until lobster is heated through.

Place rice on serving plate, and sprinkle with chives.

Remove lobster from frypan retaining the cooking liquid as a sauce.

Arrange the lobster on the rice and spoon sauce, which has been
cooked with the lobster, over lobster. Serve with lemon wedges
on side of plate.

INGREDIENTS

4 tbsp. butter
1 tsp. garlic, crushed
2 spring onions, chopped
1 x 12 oz. (300 g) can tomatoes
salt and pepper, to taste
pinch of saffron
1 large cooked lobster
1 1/4 cup (10 fl. oz/297 ml) brandy
boiled rice

1/2 bunch fresh chives,
chopped, for garnish
lemon wedges, for garnish

Surf and Turf

Serves 2

PREPARATION

Place steaks on hot grill and cook to your liking.
Remove to heated serving plates, keep warm.

Remove flesh from lobster tail and cut into pieces.
Heat butter in a fry pan and cook garlic
for 1–2 minutes. Add lobster and parsley
to pan and cook for 3–4 minutes
over a medium high heat.

Spoon lobster and butter over each steak
and serve with grilled asparagus.

INGREDIENTS

2 Porterhouse steaks
2 tbsp. butter
2 cloves garlic, finely chopped
1 tbsp. chopped parsley
1 large lobster tail

Lobster Sweet and Sour

86

PREPARATION

To make the court bouillon in which to cook the lobster combine white wine, all the vegetables except the shallots (prepared and cut in pieces), the bouquet garni, 1 ½ teaspoon coarse sea salt, a few peppercorns, and water. Prepare the lobster, add to the boiling court bouillon, and cook gently for about 30 minutes. Drain well and when slightly cooler, cut lengthwise down the middle. Remove the flesh carefully, reserving the shells.

Peel and finely chop the shallots, fry in 3 tablespoons butter and 3 tablespoons oil; add the sparkling wine and reduce by half; blanch, peel, and seed the tomatoes, chop and add to the pan. Boil for 10 minutes, uncovered, to reduce and thicken, and season with salt and pepper. Add the sugar, simmer for 10 minutes more, then add the lobster flesh (still in two halves).
Stir gently while cooking in the sauce for 5 minutes.

Use a slotted spoon to remove the lobster halves from the sauce and replace them in the half shells, on a heated serving plate.
Coat them with a little sauce and serve the rest in a sauceboat.

INGREDIENTS

1 lobster about 2 1/2 (1 kg)
2 1/4 cups (18 fl. oz./500 ml) dry white wine
2 carrots
2 celery stalks
1 onion
1 bouquet garni
2 shallots
3 tbsp. butter
3 tbsp. oil
7/8 cup (7 fl. oz./207 ml) sparkling white wine
14 oz. (400 g) ripe tomatoes

1 tsp. sugar
salt and peppercorns

NOTE

Serve with a mixed salad.

Lobster Sashimi
(Ise Ebi)

PREPARATION

If lobster is purchased frozen, allow to defrost overnight
in the refrigerator.

Remove the head and reserve for garnish.

Use poultry scissors to make a nice clean cut in the tail shell.

Pull the lobster meat out. Stuff the empty shell with shredded daikon
radish for presentation. Cut the lobster into small sashimi slices.

Lay the meat on the daikon bedded tail, and serve.

INGREDIENTS

1 whole green (uncooked) lobster
endive, shredded carrot
shredded daikon radish

NOTE

Traditionally, lobsters that were to be
prepared as sashimi were purchased live
and killed moments before being presented
and served. The Japanese obsession
with absolute freshness made this practice
commonplace.

Seafood Pizza

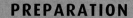

PREPARATION

Spread crust with tomato sauce, add vegetables and seafood,
top with cheese.

Place in the oven on the rack. Cook on low heat, until cheese melts,
and pizza is heated through.

INGREDIENTS

Ready-to-bake pizza crust
pasta sauce
mushrooms
chopped mixed vegetables
grated cheese (combine mozzarella,
Cheddar, and Monterey Jack)
A variety of cooked seafood
(mussels, lobster meat, crab meat,
flaked fish, clams, et.)

Tarragon Seafood Salad

Serves 4

INGREDIENTS

4 tbsp. chopped fresh tarragon,
2 tbsp. lime juice
3 tbsp. grated lime rind
1 fresh red chili, chopped
2 tsp. olive oil
freshly ground black pepper
1 lb. (500 g) uncooked lobster tail,
flesh removed from shell
and cut into
large pieces or 1 lb. (500 g) firm

white fish filets, cut into large pieces
8 oz. (250 g) snow pea sprouts or
watercress
1 cucumber, sliced into ribbons
2 carrots, sliced into ribbons
1 red bell pepper,
cut into thin strips

PREPARATION

Place tarragon, lime juice, lime rind, chili, oil and black pepper to taste in a bowl and mix to combine. Add lobster, toss to coat and set aside to marinate for 15 minutes.

Arrange snow pea sprouts or watercress, cucumber, carrot, and red bell pepper on a large serving platter and set aside.

Heat grill or frying pan over a high heat, add lobster mixture and cook, turning frequently, for 2 minutes or until lobster is tender. Arrange lobster over salad, spoon over pan juices and serve immediately.

NOTE

To make cucumber and carrot ribbons, use a vegetable peeler to remove strips lengthwise from the cucumber or carrot. This salad is also delicious made using shrimp instead of lobster. If using shrimp, shell and devein them before marinating.

Rock Lobster and Smoked Ocean Trout Salad

PREPARATION

Remove the meat from the tail of the rock lobster, slice finely,
and set aside. Alternatively, ask your fishmonger to do this for you.
Cut the smoked ocean trout into thin strips and also set aside.
Slice the cucumber in half, lengthways and scoop out and discard
the seeds. Slice on a mandoline or "V-slicer" (or use a vegetable peeler)
to make long, skinny strips resembling fettuccine. Peel the carrot
and slice in the same manner as the cucumber. Keeping the zucchini
whole, also slice them lengthways into long thin strips.

Mix together the lobster, ocean trout, vegetables, and tatsoi leaves
gently. For the dressing, heat the lime juice and dissolve the palm sugar.
Pour into a bowl and whisk in the olive oil until the mixture is thick
and the oil has emulsified with the lime juice. Season with salt
and pepper and mix this through the salad ingredients.
Arrange the salad in an attractive platter and sprinkle the chives over.

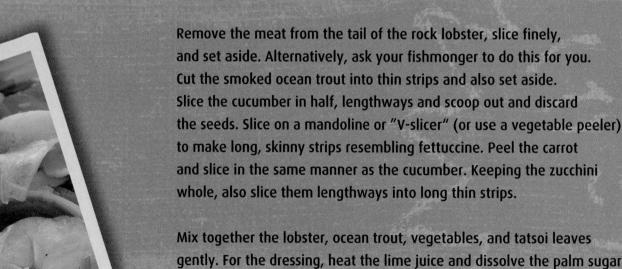

INGREDIENTS

1 cooked rock lobster
14 oz. (400 g) smoked ocean trout
1 continental cucumber, 1 carrot
1 green zucchini, 1 yellow zucchini
3 1/2 oz. (100 g) tatsoi leaves
1 bunch chives, snipped

DRESSING

juice of 2 limes, 1 tbsp. palm sugar
1/2 cup (4 fl. oz./120 ml) olive oil,
salt and pepper

Index

96